That's Not a Pet!

CAN I HAVE A PET POLAR BEAR?

By Bert Wilberforce

Gareth Stevens
PUBLISHING

Please visit our website, www.garethstevens.com. For a free color catalog of all our high-quality books, call toll free 1-800-542-2595 or fax 1-877-542-2596.

Library of Congress Cataloging-in-Publication Data

Names: Wilberforce, Bert, author.
Title: Can I have a pet polar bear? / Bert Wilberforce.
Description: New York : Gareth Stevens Publishing, [2019] | Series: That's not a pet! | Includes index.
Identifiers: LCCN 2017040519| ISBN 9781538218006 (library bound) | ISBN 9781538218020 (pbk.) | ISBN 9781538218037 (6 pack)
Subjects: LCSH: Polar bear–Juvenile literature. | Pets–Juvenile literature.
Classification: LCC QL737.C27 W553 2019 | DDC 599.786–dc23
LC record available at https://lccn.loc.gov/2017040519

First Edition

Published in 2019 by
Gareth Stevens Publishing
111 East 14th Street, Suite 349
New York, NY 10003

Editor: Therese Shea
Designer: Sarah Liddell

Photo credits: Cover, p. 1 Sergey Uryadnikov/Shutterstock.com; p. 5 Chase Dekker/Shutterstock.com; p. 7 Alexey Seafarer/Shutterstock.com; p. 9 Lars Kristensen/EyeEm/EyeEm/Getty Images; pp. 11, 24 (claw) Nagel Photography/Shutterstock.com; p. 13 NaturesMomentsuk/Shutterstock.com; p. 15 Galina Savina/Shutterstock.com; p. 17 Jan Martin Will/Shutterstock.com; pp. 19, 24 (seal) vladsilver/Shutterstock.com; p. 21 Nirut Sampan/Shutterstock.com; p. 23 SEBASTIEN BOZON/Stringer/AFP/Getty Images.

Printed in the United States of America

CPSIA compliance information: Batch #CS18GS: For further information contact Gareth Stevens, New York, New York at 1-800-542-2595.

Contents

I want a pet.
I want a polar bear!

Polar bears are big bears.
They live in the Arctic.

They have fur
to keep warm.
They have black skin
under it.

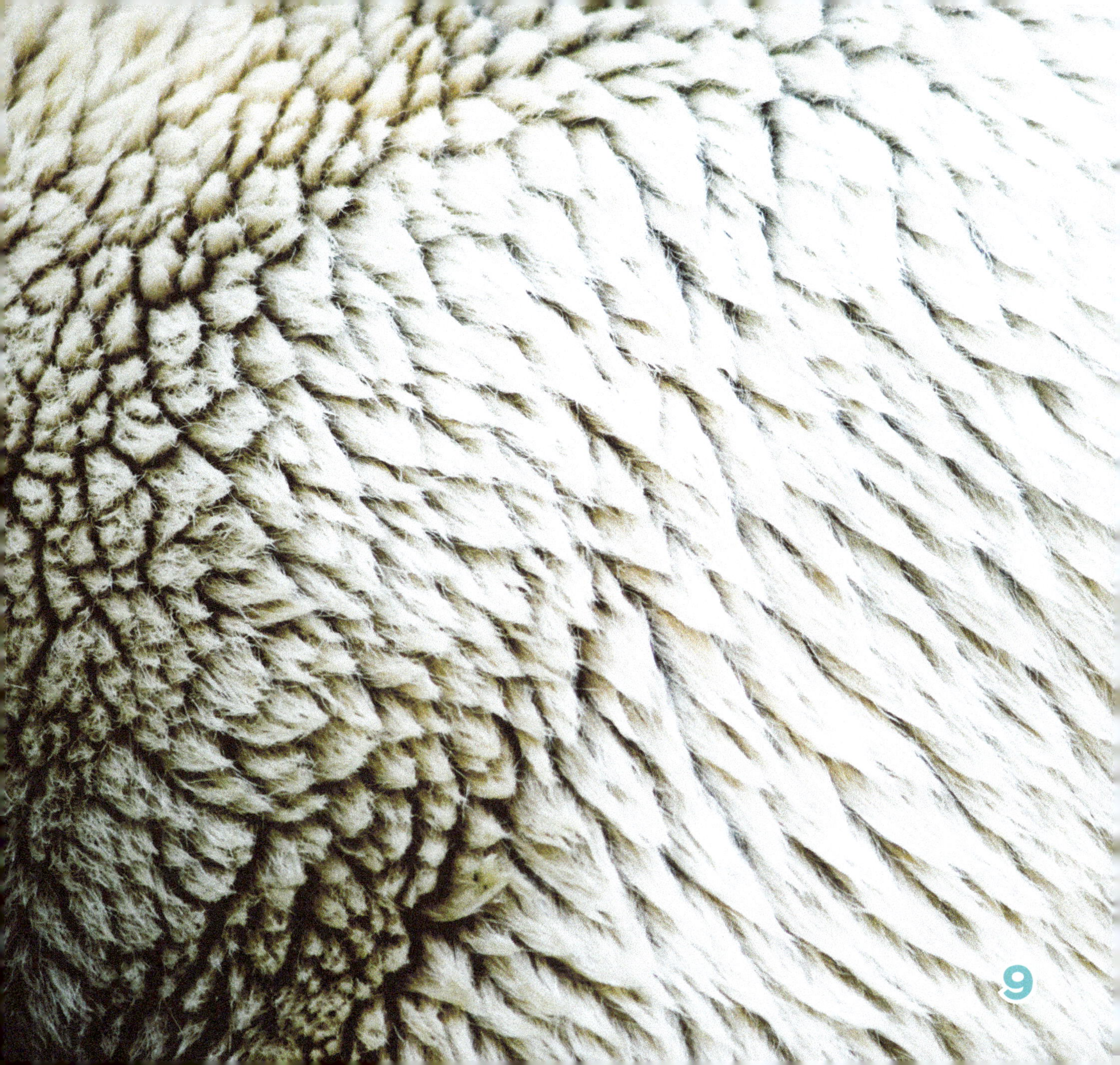

Polar bears have sharp claws.

They can run on ice.
They dig, too.

Polar bears can swim for hours!

They float on ice, too!

They look for animals
to eat.
They hunt seals.

Polar bears are fierce!
They aren't good pets.

I'll see them at the zoo!

Words to Know

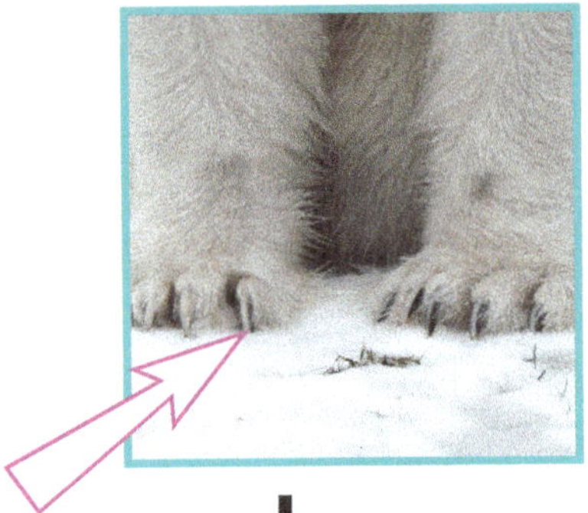

claw

seal

Index